GREECE

IN COLOUR

EDITIONS K. GOUVOUSSIS

5 ODOS RATZIERI - ATHENS - GREECE

GREECE

Andre Gide once said that to try to dissect a classical myth in search of its inner meaning is like shattering the Horn of Plenty in order to find the secret of its abundance. You end up with a pile of ornamental fragments, and your quest for the truth is no further advanced. He could have used same simile for the attempt to define Greece itself, the mother of the myths. Greece is a synthesis of geography, history, art, architecture and poetry, an antithesis of simplicity and sophistication, the link between East and West and yet entirely separate from either, a country in which the past lives on indistinguishably interwoven with the present. To see this country in terms of its individual components is to admire the ornamental fragments without grasping their significance. Greece must be experienced, as the Greeks themselves experience it, intensely; you must live and absorb it from every aspect and then perhaps you will understand it.

Even each tiny component contains its own contrast. Geographically for example, Greece falls into two distinct sectors; the mainland itself, which forms the south-easternmost extension of the Balkan peninsula, and the islands, from Corfu in the west to Samos in the east, from Thassos in the north to Crete in the south. Four countries touch its northern borders, Albania, Yugoslavia, Bulgaria and Turkey, three seas wash its immense coastline, the Ionian, Mediterranean and Aegaean. A mountainous land for four-fifths of its extent, the highest range is the home of the archaic gods, Olympos, which towers to over 9,500 feet, in parts gentle and wooded, in others naked and harsh, here sudden and precipitous, there long and sweeping. Yet at the foot of this very symbol of Greek mountains lies its antithesis, the great plain of Thessaly, stretching for some 500 square miles, flat and fertile, known since Homer as the breader of horses, where the dark North wind himself comes down to mate with the brood mares. And through this great plain flows one of the larger rivers of Greece, the Penios, a flurry of cataracts in the upper reaches of its 135 miles, typically swift, shallow and unnavigable in its lower course. The islands, too, show a similar vivid variation of scenery. To set out from the rich greenery of Samos or Mytilene and come upon the bare rocks of the Cyclades is indeed to pass from one world to another Thassos with its forests, summer rainstorms, and streams which brim all year round, belongs essentially to the Balkan scenery of neighbouring Macedonia. Rhodes, with its dry luminous summers, spreading vineyards, the heavy scent of pine woods, the delicacy of mimosa, the abundance of butterflies is essentially a last challenge of the Mediterranean flung in the face of Asia, as though the Knights of St. John had, to nullify their expulsion, subtly metamorphosed it into a mirror their western homelands.

Throughout this geographical kaleidoscope is scattered a population approaching nine million people, each region with its own traditions and crafts, its own accent and idioms of speech. Two million of them are gathered into the city of Athens, one of the gayest and most extravert capitals of Europe, and into the Piraeus, a vigorous port and focal point of the national mercantile tradition. Again, how the contrasts haunt us. To leave the sun scorched threshing floors of the Peloponese or the taciturn tobacco-growers of Macedonia and to find oneself among the night-clubs and tavernas of the Plaka or watching the sophisticated gaiety of the young Piraeots is not simply to move from place to place, it is to step out of one age into another. And yet, fundamentally, it is all Greece and they are all Greeks, a mysterious and deep bond of national consciousness that renders the apparent divisions superficial.

The name of Athens is for many foreigners identified with the concept of Greece itself, yet it has held its position of central power only for a very short period of the history of the country. The roots of the Hellenic tradition, and of the European civilisation which indirectly derived from it, lie far to the southeast, in Crete, where from about 2000 B.C. onwards, a ruling house bearing, according to legend, the style of «Minos» reigned over a broad and peaceful empire whose opulence is typified in the complex splendour of the palace at Knossos (near modern Heraklion). This era was brought to an end in about 1400 B.C. by a disaster of an unknown nature. Athenian propagandists of a later age attributed it to Theseus, son of the King of Athens, who slew the terrible Minotaur, half bull, half man, in the Labyrinth and ended the obligation of the mainland to pay tribute to Minos. Here we can trace something of the cloudy prosess by which history becomes legend. The Labyrinth is a poetical transmutation of the memories of the complex of corridors and underground passages in the Knossos palace, and in the concept of the Minotaur there is a confused reference to the bull dances shown on frescoes now in the Heraklion Museum. Modern archaeology finds it more probable that the catastrophe was connected with a terrible earthquake on the volcanic island of Santorini where exciting new finds are being excavated that may throw light on the mystery.

From Crete the hegemony of the empire passed to the High King of Mycenae, in the north east Peloponnese, who must have been at the apogee of his power about the time of the fall of Troy (1194 B.C.). Here we are once more in the land of myth. The monarch that sailed across the Aegean to help his brother regain «the face that launched a thousand ships» was none other than the ill-fated Agamemnon, destined to die on his return at the hands of his adulterous wife Clytemnaestra, who in her turn was despatched by their son Orestes, a story that has fascinated dramatists from Aeschylus to Sartre. But invasions from the north eventually destroyed this empire too, and it was not until the rise of Athens in the 5th century B.C., its decisive rejection of the Persian threat, and the foundation of its great maritime empire that a unified force manifested itself again. By defeating the Persians, first on the plains of Marathon in 490 B.C., then at the sea battle of Salamis ten years later, Athens acquired an apparently unshakeable position among the city states of Greece. Under Pericles' leadership the city entered what is known as the Golden Age, famous for its architecture, playwrights and philosophers. With the spoils of Marathon and Salamis the Athenians could institute the ambitious building programme which has given us, amongst other things, the glories of the Parthenon. It was the age of Aeschylus' incantatory verse, of Praxiteles' sculptured hymns to the perfect male form, of Plato distilling the essence of his master's thought beside the plane trees of the Ilyssus. All the known world attended the great games at Olympia. All the known word listened attentively to the voice of the great oracle at Delphi. Greece was united and flourishing. But the rift in the lute was not long in appearing. The Spartans had immortalised the spirit of defiant Hellenism in the famous heroic stand at Thermopylae in 480 B.C., when their king Leonidas with his 300 followers and a few picked allies defended the pass against a countless Persian host, until, betrayed by a spy, they died, fighting, where they stood.But the Spartan dedication to a military ideal was so at variance with both the spiritual and the territorial aims of Athens that eventually the two powers became locked in mortal conflict. What together they had saved, together they destroyed, and the balance of power passed into the hands of the strange half-Greek, half-barbarian dynasty of Philip II of Macedon and his wild adventurous son Alexander the Great, who ruled from

Pella (about 40 miles from Thessaloniki). Alexander carried the banner of Greek civilisation right across the Middle East into India (336-323 B.C.) in one of the most successful cultural crusades of all time. When his armies withdrew, what they stood for remained. So deep was the memory of Alexander's power that even now in modern folklore the sailors relate how, occasionaly, a mermaid will appear on the prow of a fishing boat and ask whether Alexander still lives and reigns. To reassure her of the fact is enough to ensure a safe voyage. Otherwise she will stir up a vicious storm and probably send the boat to the bottom.

From Pella, the focus of Greek civilisation passed out of Greece altogether, to Alexandria in Egypt. Political power had vanished to be replaced by a cultural infiltration of the whole Mediterranean. Rome rose and fell, but its gods, its philosophy, its literature were absorbed into a Greek mould, and it was a Roman emperor, Constantine, who set up the strange orientalised Christian empire at Byzantium (Constantinople) which was to last almost twice as long as its Roman predecessor. In the classical period the Greek cities of Asia Minor had been centres of elegant and sophisticated civilization. With the expansion of the Byzantine Empire they returned to their own. Foreigners often fail to appreciate the importance of this epoch in the history of Greece, but the statically gorgeous hieratic art that is preserved in so many mosaics and frescoes is as fundamental an element of the Greek heritage as the Parthenon, and the very name of Constantinople is still a symbol of the zenith of power to which Greece then attained.

All this time, what we now consider Greece was a relatively unimportant province. It came to the forefront again in an odd way. In 1204 the Frankish armies of the Fourth Crusade inexcusably and barbarously sacked Constantinople and carved up the Empire for themselves. Their sway in the capital itself lasted a mere handful of decades, but many of the curious duchies and principalities they set up (echoed in the exotic titles of Shakespearian characters, like the Duke of Athens) lived on for over two hundred years, The principality of the Morea, covering most of the Peloponnese except for the wild isolated Mani peninsula in the south, lasted under the Villehardouins and the House of Savoy right until 1450 when it finally succumbed to Venetian encroachments and the subtle negotiations of the new imperial rulers of Byzantium. A handful of impressive castles remains to mark this era, often in very beautiful situations, like the Fortress on Acrocorinth, Khlemoutsi (near Kyllini in the west Peloponnese) or the little castle at Karitaina (near Andritsaina). Fascinating too are the Byzantine town at Mistra, the Renaissance houses at Monemvasia and the pecariously perched rock monasteries of the Meteora, strange fragments of another age clinging tenaciously in an alien world.

As if the historical threads, Cretan, Mycenaean, Athenian, Byzantine and Frankish, were not sufficiently complex already, the moment was fast approaching for the superimposition of two further influences in the development of Greece, those of Turkey and Venice. Undermined and impoverished, the Bysantine Empire never recovered from the Frankish interlude. Though in its last moments it bequeathed an artistic heritage to the west that was profoundly to influence Giotto, and a wealth of literary and philosophical material on which was nurtured the classical revival in Italy, it was essentially a dying civilisation waiting for the Sultan at its gate. Probably the greatest of modern Greek poets, Costis Palamas, has a moving passage in his poem, The Twelve Lays of the Gipsy, in which he describes the treasures of classical Greece being shipped to the west as the great golden gates of the City swing open of their own accord to receive the Turks. Byzantium was a ripe fruit and in 1453 it fell.

But the Turks were not to have their own way entirely. The marine power of the Doges was to dispute with the Sublime Porte for decades, and in some areas centuries, a struggle during the course of which a Venetian shell, in 1687, landed in the Turkish powder magazine, in the Parthenon, and tragically destroyed a large part of what was until then an almost perfect building. In Crete, Venetian domination lasted until, after a 24-year siege, Heraklion finally fell in 1669. And in the Ionian islands, Venice's sway yielded only to the French and later the British occupation. It was in these Italianised regions, paradoxically, that modern Greek literature, in the form of the Cretan Renaissance and later the poetry of Dionyssios Solomos, found its first expression, while the in someways less oppressed lands of the Turkish occupation were still in a state of complete cultural inertia.

After the Greek War of Independence (1821) a temporary capital was set up at the charming old town of Nafplion (1829-34), it was there that the Assembly of 1832 confirmed the election of the first King, Otto of Bavaria, to the Greek throne, and it was the garrison of that town that in 1862 gave the signal for the rising against the same wretched monarch.

So finally, Athens came into its own. But an Athens very different from the modern city, a mere cluster of little houses at the foot of the Acropolis. covering roughly the area of the present Plaka. As late as the 1920s when the comparatively sophisticated refugees from Asia Minor and Pontos arrived, they were to find the Piraeus hardly more than a large fishing harbour and surrounded by a few hersmen whose womenfolk still covered their faces in public. The Second World war hastened the process of urban development which the arrival of the refugees had begun and the city is now a vast complex of modern buildings, amid which the symbols of the classical and the Byzantine epocks stand undisconcerted.

It's often forgotten that the Greece which became independent in 1832 was only a truncated fragment of the present country. The Ionian Islands were handed over in 1864 as an accession present from Great Britain to the second King, George I. The revision of the frontiers in 1881, which contributed a further 13,395 square miles of central Greece to the new kingdom, still left most of Thessaly and all Macedonia and Thrace in foreign hands. It was only through the first Balkan War (against Turkey) in 1912, and the second (against Bulgaria) in 1913, that these territories plus Crete and the bulk of the Aegaean islands became part of Greece. Indeed Rhodes and the other islands of the Dodecanese were not finally liberated (from the Italians) until after the Second World War. It is difficult for the foreigner to believe that Yannina and Thessaloniki, those essentially Greek cities, were still under foreign domination scarcely more than a half century ago.

No race could be more fervently aware of its national identity (in the best possible sense of that phrase) than the Greeks of today. They have achieved the extension of their territory to include all but the former Greek areas of Asia Minor and Pontos and the islands of Tenedos and Imbros (and they might have had these areas too, but for the suicidal military manoeuvres of the then king, which precipitated the Asia Minor disaster of 1922).

The palaces of Crete and Mycenae, the great classical shrines of Delphi and Olympia, the Byzantine churches and monasteries such as Daphni and Osios Loukas, the castles of the Morea, are an everyday reminder of their historical continuity. Great festivals of classical drama every year still take place in the ancient theatres of Dodoni, Epidavros and Herodes Atticus (Athens). The language which the people speak has developed uninterruptedly for over 2,500 years from the days in which the Homeric poems were composed. It is still capable of produc ing fine literature, the novels of Kazantsakis, the poetry of Palamas, Sikelianos and Cavafy, equal to the greatest works of contemporary European writers, but so fundamentally Greek that they almost defy translation.

The Greeks themselves are friendly and lively with an almost un-limited capacity for enjoying themselves, helped by the fact that their concept of human relations is refreshingly uncomplicated. Much of their system of values has remained unchanged since pre-classical times, faithfulness to friends, respect for the obligations of hospitality, the cult of the beautiful and a pagan sense of the remorselessness of fate. They often show an inquisitveness which the more reserved northern races can mistake for impertinence but which is simply a manifestation of their natural interest in the world around them. It is rare to find a Greek who lacks awareness of the fascination of life in a very physical sense. Music andt dancing too are an essential part of their lives and it is noticeable that the young, though capable exponents, after their own style, of western dances, are also devoted to their own dances, To see a well-executed hasapiko or the more acrobatic zembekiko is an experience which never palls with repetition. Against all this, is the aspect which the northerner finds the most difficult to assimilate, the Greek sense of time. The rhythm of their life is essentially Mediterranean.

Everything is promised with the best intentions; if it doesn't materia-lise there is no cause for worry. The world will still be with us tomorrow.

This air of extemporising from moment to moment can be infuriating but it can also be charming. Like the habit of the siesta, one is likely to absorb it oneself without noticing.

Despite the Greek love of improvisation, moving from place to place presents little problem, as the country now has a quite well-developed, modern system of internal communications. Aside from the international railway that runs down through Thessaloniki to Athens there is also the little railway that circles the Peloponnese, including most of the tourist areas in its orbit. Buses are organised in both local and cross country networks, and for very long distances, like Thessaloniki to Athens. It is advisable to book in advance. As for boats, there is constant traffic between the Piraeus and the nearby islands of the Saronic Gulf, most of the further islands of any size are served by a daily boat with caiques to link the smaller islands, and there are also regular services between Greece and Italy and the Western Mediterranean. Sea travel is relatively inexpensive, and, in the warm starry nights of midsummer, becomes a pleasure in itself. Internal air services too have been established by Olympic Airways linking Athens with eighteen islands and cities. including Thessaloniki, Yannina and Larissa, Chanea and Hiraklion (in Crete), and the islands of Samos, Mytilene, Cos, Rhodes and Corfu.

For those who want a balanced holiday, sun and sea, culture and relaxation, Greece is the perfect country. Whether you want to swim or just laze on the sand, alone or in company, you will find plenty of locations to your taste. There are organised beaches like those just outside Athens at Glyfada (10 miles) and Vouliagmeni (15 miles), with changing rooms, showers, restaurants and sports facilities; there are tiny rocky bays for diving and underwater fishing especially along the Gulf of Corinth; and the islands are noted for their gently shelving bays with long sweeping stretches of clear sand. Sometimes a site combines the best of both worlds, as cape Sounion, at the end of the Attica peninsula, with its rocky deep water bay to the left and its sandy beach to the right the whole dominated by the exquisite Temple of Poseidon.

Accommodation too is being brought rapidly up to date. In the major centres, there is now a large range of hotels, classified from AA to E and covering a wide spectrum of prices. In some rural areas, Village Guest houses have been set up with modest but cheap facilities, and, particularly in the islands, there are plenty of rooms available in private houses. There are also a limited number of motels, holiday camps and organised camping sites. It is a long way from the sweeping modern architecture of the National Tourist Organisation-sponsored chain of Xenia hotels to the dazzling white, pink and blue cubes of the island houses that cling like toys to their grey-green rocks. The relative importance of comfort and romantic atmosphere, not to mention price, will dictate the individual's choice.

The question of food and drink can be a stumbling block to the unwary. Both Greek cuisine and Greek wine are often unreasonably slighted by the so-called expert. It is true that one should not make exaggerated claims for either. The cooking is limited in range, and being based on oil as opposed to butter, sacrifices subtlety to savouriness, with the result that the things to eat in Greece which the foreigner most readily appreciates, are the simple things, squid, prawns and meat roasted on the spit. The everyday needs of the tourist can be easily catered for. A straightforward rule of thumb is to pick an establishment principally patronised by Greeks and to choose the food by inspecting it in the kitchen (the Greeks do this too). But to find «haute cuisine» is rather more difficult. This is not to say that Greek food does not have an identity of its own, or that the tradition of fine cooking so famous in classical times has not been continued. But it is not a country of restaurants, and the often excellent standards of home cooking are rarely maintained outside because eating-out is regarded as either an unfortunate necessity or as a mere ancillary to some other pleasure. Unless you succumb to the easy way out, and patronise the «smart» establishments that serve indifferent international food, only the specific recommendation of local friends can really be relied on.

As for the wines, there are never likely to find high favour with the connoisseur's palate, but they are infinitely more pleasant (and cheaper) than the average table wines of France and Italy. The curious pine-flavoured wine, retsina, is an acquired taste, but after the initial shock is an admirable drink and the squeamish can always douse it with a little soda watter. The main error is to compare Greek products with their French or Italian equivalent. The brandy, for example, tastes nothing like champagne cognac, but at its best (and it is not all firewater) it is a smooth rich drink of the same quality. Likewise, Greek vermouth is very different from Martini, but none the less palatable. One wishes perhaps that, like ouzo, the aniseed spirit much consumed in every cafe and bar of the country, they simply had distinctive names which did not invite irrelevant comparisons.

Particularly in Athens, there is no lack of entertainment. The cinemas which, like many cafes and restaurants, mostly move into the open air for the summer months, show a wide range of foreign films, though the theatres, of course, are only for those with a good knowledge of Greek. Night clubs run from the sophisticated western floor show type to those patronised by the younger element with a good group and plenty of dancing. They are in the main very reasonably priced and there is no compulsion to consume a lot of alcohol, the Greeks themselves being very moderate drinkers. There are also the tavernas, restaurants with a small group playing Greek music; if it's a really Greek taverna, somebody from time to time will be moved to get up and dance his heart out. For Greek music and dancing, here are, too, the bouzouki establishments where the finest exponents of this individual instrument are to be heard . And most of the leading Greek singers are performing at a boite or night clud during the summer. The bulk of these establishments are clustered together in the Plaka area just at the foot of the Acropolis or strung along the Attica coast from the Pireaus down towards Vouliagmeni. The wine-dark Aegaean on a starry night may be a cliche but it is still irresistably beautiful, and many people favour the coastal night clubs and the excellent waterfront restaurants of the Piraeus, because of the extra romantic fillip that view across the sea provides.

Greece, above all, is a country for the inquisitive visitor who is not afraid to explore, to test, to submerge himself in a world of strange and new experiences, to absorb and let himself be absorbed. It is wasted on those who want life brought to them neatly packaged in cellophane. Somewhere in this vast synthesis of time, space, light and colour, vibrant with the high spirits of the present, suspended in the sublime calm of the past, every thinking man will find the image of himself that he is seeking.

Bird's eye view of the Acropolis of Athens (Restoration)

Aerial view of the Acropolis

THE ACROPOLIS

The Acropolis or (high city) is a rocky hill 156 m. above sea level, dominating the centre of the town. It is a true natural fortress since it is inaccessible from all sides except the west side where the entrance is located.

From the earliest times it had been both a fortress and the religious centre of the state. The principal cult was that of the goddess Athena and in her honour were constracted on the Acropolis splendid temples.

The most remarkable monuments: the Parthenon, the Erechtheion, the Propylaea, and the temple of Nike were built in the last half of the 5th century B.C. under the inspiration of Pericles and even in ruins witness «the glory that was Greece».

The Acropolis seen from the hill of Pnyx

The Propylaea of the Acropolis

THE PROPYLAEA

The monumental gate was conceived and executed by the architect Mnesicles as «the radiant diadem of the citadel of the gods» between 437 and 432 B.C. Never quite completed because of the outbreak of the Peloponnesian War, the only opening in the encircling walls extends over 150 feet divided into a central portico and two asymmetrical wings, in two shades of marble and two orders of architecture, Doric outside and Ionian within.

The Parthenon. Eastern facade

THE PARTHENON

The Parthenon, built on the highest part of the Acropolis, is the most important creation of ancient Greek architecture and a symbol of the perfection that marked the classical spirit of the age of Pericles — 5th century B.C. — the «Golden Age» of Greek history. It was built during the period 447-438 B.C. by the architects Ictinus and Callicrates. The composition and sculpture of its ornamentations were the work of the great Phidias, who was also the co-ordinator of the whole plan.

An eternal symbol of aesthetic perfection, this temple was dedicated to the goddess Athena, the Patroness of Athens. Of Doric order, the temple was made of marble extracted from Mt. Pendeli. Its length is 69.51 m. and its width 30.87 m. Although partly ruined today — largely due to the bombardment by Morozini in 1687 — it still fills the visitor with admiration and awe.

THE ERECTHEION

In this area are found the oldest and most sacred relics of ancient Athens, the mycenean palace, the tomb and shrine of Kekrops, the marks of Poseidon's trident, the sacred olive tree of Athena.

All these contributed and so the building has such a complicated plan. It was built between 421 and 406 B.C.

The basic plan is a rectangle with three porches in different levels. So in the interior we have two sanctuaries, one dedicated to Poseidon Erechtheus which was entered from the N. and one dedicated to Athena Polias which was entered from the E. The S. porch has six statues of Korai- It is an ionic edifice with rich and elegant decoration and perfect elaboration of sur faces.

THE CARYATIDES

Caryatids on the Erechtheion

The most interesting part of the Erechtheion is the south Portico of the Caryatides or Maidens. Six statues of beautiful girls of outstanding craftsmanship. The colonnade exudes flexibility and charm. The figures stand four in front and two behind and they support an entablature like columns. The capitals of their heads are designed like baskets. Each rests her weight on the leg farthest from the center of the façade, and all produce the impression of ease and stability. The second Caryatid of the colonnade facing west is a copy plaster. The original was taken by Lord Elgin to London in 1801.

The name caryatides given to these figures in later times was derived from the town of Caryae, in Laconia.

The «Mourning Athena»

Horsemen. Slab from the North Side of the Parthenon frieze

Archaic Kore

THE ACROPOLIS MUSEUM

In the Acropolis Museum are exhibited sculptures and other finds from the Acropolis. At the present moment the Museum consists of IX Rooms. The Visitor may see sculptures of the archaic period (6th century), the classical period and a few of Hellenistic and Roman periods.

THE THEATRE OF DIONYSUS

The Theatre of Dionysus (south
ern slope of the Acropolis).
As early as the 6th century the
official Athenian theatre was on
this site, forming part of the great
sanctuary of Dionysus, during who
festival plays were performed. It
was here that the works of Aescy-
lus, Sophocles, Euripides and Ari-
stophanes were first performed,
though much of the stone work
of the extant building actually da-
tes from the start of the 4th C.B.
C. Apart from its artistic function,
it was also used for public meet-
ings.

The theatre of Dionysus

Odeum of Herod Atticus.

ODEON OF HERODES ATTICUS

as built in 161 A. D. by Herodes
cus in memory of his wife Regilla
served as a theatre and concert
It has 32 rows of seats which
hold 5.000 spectators.
ording to Philostratos the Odeon
covered with a wooden roof.

The Acropolis illuminated

The Athens Festival of Music and Drama is held every summer with the participation of the world's greatest conductors, soloists, orchestras, theatre and ballet companies in the Theatre of Herodes Atticus. The Greek Royal Theatre presents ancient tragedies and commedies, which are also performed in the Lycabettus Theatre, while the Philopappus Theatre is given over to folk dancing.
The «Sound and Light» performances on the Pnyx highlight the great moments in the history of the Acropolis.

The Parthenon from the Propylaea at night

▼ *Odeum of Herod Atticus*

THE AREOPAGUS

On the rocky knoll below the Propylaea, Ares, the God of War, was judged by his Olympian peers for the slaying of Poseidon's son. This legendary precedence made the Areopagus, the Hill of Ares, the first court of homicide to which Orestes appealed when pursued by the Furies for the murder of his mother.

Saint Paul preached from this natural pulpit and converted a senator who was canonized and as Saint Dionysius Areopagite became the patron of Athens.

The Bema in the Pnyx

THE MONUMENT
OF PHILOPAPPUS

The highest hill (481 feet) facing the Acropolis is crowned by the ruined marble monument of Philopappus, a Syrian prince and Roman consul, honoured by the Athenians in 116 A.-D. for his gifts to their city.

Pericles addressing the Athenians on the hill of Pnyx

CERAMICOS

In Ceramicos, the illustrious Athenian were buried by the state, particularly those who had fallen in battle. Their tombs were made on either side of great road leading to Academy.

THE MONUMENT OF LYSISTRATES

This 4th-century B.-C. choragic nument, one of many that once l the street of the Tripods from town to the theatre of Dionysus. tiny cylindrical edifice of Pen marble rises 21 feet above its b The frieze depicts the defeat of Tyrrhenian pirates by Diony

TOWER OF WINDS

The 1st century B.C. Tower of the Winds was a gift of Andronicus Cyrrhestes, a hydraulic clock with a sun dial and weather vane.

Theseion

The Theseum (correctly called the Hephaisteum as it was consecrated to the god Hephaistos) is the most intact of all the known Greek temples. A mixture of Doric and Ionic elements, it is probably slightly older than the Parthenon. It stands on a slight rise overlooking the extensive remain of the ancient market-place (agora) at the north-west foot of the acropolis, and facing the restored Roman stoa of Attalos.

The temple of Olympian Zeus

THE TEMPLE OF ZEUS AND THE ARCH OF HADRIAN

Hadrian completed the temple of Olympian Zeus about 700 years after Peisistratus had raised the first immense columns — 7 feet 10 inches in diameter. The 104 Corinthian marble columnus of the Roman sanctuary were a third smaller, though still the largest in Europe, as was the temple itself, 354 by 135 feet. The Roman general Sulla removed the pillars of the intervening Hellenistic temple to Rome in the first century B.C.; Genoese and Venetians did likewise with Hadrian's marbles, so that only 16 columns now remain 13 standing together under their architraves.

The slender arch consisting of an apsis decorated with Corinthian columns proclaims on the western side «This is the city of Theseus» and on the eastern «This is the city of Hadrian». Hadrian indeed greatly enlarged the town and established entire new quarters north of the temple of Zeus.

The Arch of Hadrian

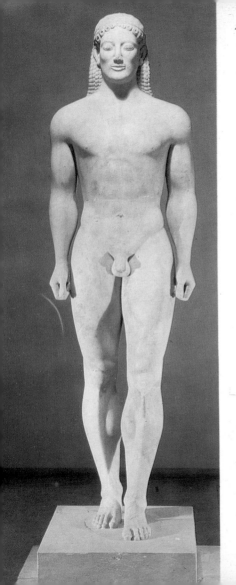

Kouros

Cycladic art.

GREEK ARCHAEOLOGICAL TREASURES IN THE MUSEUMS

Close to all the main classical sites are museums containing the priceless heritage of the plastic arts that has been saved from Greece's great past; sculpture, temple friezes, frescoes, pottery and jewellery of all ages, from the angular and quasi abstract decorations on the vases of the geometric period through to the overripe curves and lush realism of Hellenistic and Greco-Roman statuary. By far the biggest and most dazzling collections is in the National Archaeological Museum in Athens (Odos 28 Oktovriou). Most famous are the Mycenaean gold work including the death mask of Agamemnon, the strange archaic figures from the Cyclades that call to mind the techniques of modern sculpture, the preclassical kouroi (youths), and the sculpture of the golden age, famous for its nobility and perfection of line, as in the Youth of Anticythera or the bronze statue of Zeus.

g funerary ampfora of the ripe geometric stele

The Cup from Vafio   Mask from the Acropolis of Mycenae

Bronze race horse with its small Jockey. Found in 1927 of Cape Artemision in Euboea together with the bronze statue of Poseidon. About the middle of the 2nd century B.C.

The youth of Antikythera

National Arch. Museum.

Bronze statue of Poseidon (or Zeus) 460 B.C.

THE MONASTERY OF KAISSARIANI

Of the five monasteries on Mount Hymettus, the retreat of Kaissariani — though long disaffected — is by far the most romantic. Built on a sanctuary of Aphrodite near a spring, the 11th-century hexagonal cupola supported by four Ionian columns blends harmoniously with the later narthex and campanile. The 16th-century frescoes portray the Virgin seated between the Archangels in the apse and the Apostles on the north wall.

The refectory, kitchen and some cells have been restored in the charming setting of the wooded slopes.

DAPHNI

The Emperor Justinian constructed a fortified monastery over the ruined temple of Apollo, but the church of the Assumption with its magnificent mosaics was only added some 500 years later.

The Frankish dukes invited Cistercian monks as guardians of their last resting place and two sarcophagi with fleurs-de-lis still stand in the Gothic cloisters.

When the last duke strangled his aunt before Daphni's altar, Sultan Mohammed II occupied Athens executed the duke and expelled the Cistercians. After centuries of neglect Orthodox monks returned and defended the monastery during the War of Independence. Following extensive restorations the superb mosaic of Christ Pantocrator looks again severely down on biblical scenes of astounding freedom of line and delicate colouring.

Daphni   *The Christ Mosaic in the Daphni*

The Panathenaic Stadium

THE STADIUM

This stadium, in marble, which can hold 70.000 spectators was built in 1895 (donation of Averoff) for the first modern Olympic games. It occupies the same site of the ancient Panathenaic Stadium the building of which begun under Lykurgos in 330 B.C. and was completed in 140 A.D. at the expence of Herodes Atticus the great benefactor to the city of Athens.

Evzones (Royal Guard)

The Port of Piraeus

THE PIRAEUS

A corner of the harbour at the Piraeus. The father of the Athenian navy, Themistocles, initiated the task of founding a port here at the outset of the fifth century B.C. and the construction of the famous Long Walls running down from Athens to the sea (by Kimon and Pericles) copleted his object. It at once became a cosmopolitan commercial centre, a character which the modern city has rapidly regained in the 20th century, adding to it the face of a highly developed industrial complex.

MODERN ATHENS

A view across the modern city of Athens towards Mount Lycavettos. This hill, which according to legend was thrown down by Athena when she learnt of the disobedience of the daughters of Cecrops, dominates, the town, with a panoramic view across the Piraeus to the Saronic Gulf. On the summit of the hill is the Chapel of St. George.

Aegina: Temple of Aphaia (5th Century B.C.)

SOUNION

The wind-swept cape was an obvious choice for a sanctuary of Poseidon, where the sailors might offer a last sacrifice to propitiate the mighty God of the Sea, before leaving the comparative safety of the Saronic Gulf for the perils of the open archipelago. The archaic temple was destroyed by the Persians in 480 B.C. and rebuilt like numerous other shrines throughout Attica by Pericles. The pure whiteness of the 12 remaining Doric columns is still as dazzling against the deep-blue sky as in the days of Byron who carved his name into the marble.

On a lower hill, beyond the fortifications of the Peloponnesian War, stands the temple of Athena Sounias, a simple rectangle to which Ionian colonnades were later added on two sides.

THE CORINTH CANAL

The Corinth Canal, begun 18
and completed 1893. The id
of cutting a canal through t
narrow neck of the isthmus wh
joins the Peloponnese to the r
of Greece was conceived in cl
sical times and seriously invest
ted by several Roman emperor
The present canal is 6,939 yar
long, its bed width is 75,6 as
Suez, the depth of water is 2
It shortens the voyage betwe
the Adriatic and the Piraeus
some 200 miles.

Old Corinth: Temple of Apollo

OLD CORINTH

The Temple of Apollo at Corinth, one of the oldest in Greece (epoch of Periander c. 585 B.C.). In classical times, Corinth was famous as a trading centre, and for its love of luxury and pleasures. Its maritime interest led it to its advantage into the anti-Athenian camp in the quarrels which reft Greece in the fourth century B.C. Above the site towers Acrocorinth where the famous sacred prositudes once had their temple. An imposing fortress was later built there of which extensive ruins survive and was held successively by Byzantines, Franks, Venetians and Turks. In 1208, its last Byzantine commander, Leon Sgouros, met his doom by riding his horse over the precipitous edge rather than surrender to the Franks.

MYCENAE

The Treasury of Atreus in Mycenae

Mycenae inheritor of the Cretan Empire, looks out across the Plan of Argos to the sea. Its elevated position afforded protection from surprise attacks by pirates. At the time of its power (c. 1400 B.C.) the population was grouped around the vast central fortress where the reigning family had its residence and burial place. The famous Gate of the Lions is in the north-west corner of the fortress (the design is Cretan); the passage beyond it leads to the royal graveyard where Schliemann discovered priceless treasures in 1876. Outside the fortress proper lie the impressive beehive tombs including that ascribed to Agamemnon (above). The stone over the doorway alone is reckoned to weight some 120 tons. After the burial of the head of the family, the entrance passage was completely filled with earth to prevent the plundering of the tomb.

Mycenae: The Lion Gate

The ancient theatre of Epidauros

EPIDAVROS

The ancient town of Epidavros, near the east coast of the Peloponnese, was famous as the most important centre for the worship of Aesculapius, the god of medecine. When a patient recovered after treatment by the doctor priests, he would dedicate a replica of the part of his anatomy that had been affected and the museum there contains a remarkable collection of these fascinating offerings. Within the sacred precincts were also included a stadium and a great theatre. This latter, the work of Polycleitos the Younger (late 4th century B.C.), is the best preserved of any edifice of this kind. Its seating capacity is approximately 15,000 and its acoustics are superb. A festival of ancient drama is performed there every summer by the Royal Theatre Company.

Bourdzi, the old Venetian fortress at Nauplia. Now an attractive hotel.

MISTRAS

In 1248 the Frankish Prince of Achaia, Guillaume Villehardouin, having gained complete control of the south Peloponnese, decided to set up a fortress to control the area and chose one of the foothills of the Taygetos above the Plain of Sparta. The castle was called Mistra (Myzithra in mediaeval Greek) because the hill on which it stood resembled a cheese of that name. Ten years late Guillaume was captured in Macedonia fighting against the Byzantine emperor, Michael Paleologus, and the beautiful castle, the pride of his heart, was sacrificed as part of his ransome. A Greek general was installed and the hill was transformed into a Byzantine city with mansions, churches, and monasteries that still stand today. It flourished as an intellectual centre and was very dear to the Imperial family. In the cathedral of St. Demetrius, most important of all the churches of the city, the last Emperor of Byzantium, Constantine Palaiologue, was crowned in 1449. The city fought bittely on for 8 years after the fall of Constantinople in 1453, before capitualting to the Turks.

Mistra. The Byzantine churches.

Monemvasia.

MONEMVASIA

Monemvasia (whose name means «having only one entrance») was originally almost an island, but the Byzantines strengthened its connection with the land by a causeway 164 yards long. It later passed into the hands of a succession of foreign conquerors. It is notable for its churches, Renaissance houses and fine Venetian fortifications.

METHONI

Methoni stands at the point of a promontory in the southwest Peloponnese. Along the sweep of its beautiful sandy bay runs a magnificent 13th century citadel, partly rebuilt by the Venetians in 514, and again by the French in 1828.

Methoni

About 20 miles from Gythion lies the vast and beautiful complex of the Dirou caves. In the largest, the river winds in a half mile loop through a series of chambers and corridors, decorated with the fantasy shapes of stalactites, stalagmites and water-sculptured pillars.

GYTHION

Gythion, once the port of Sparta, is the place from which to set off into the Mani, the wild and independent southernmost peninsula of the Peloponnese. The Maniots have always been marked out by their courage and by their contempt for the successive masters of the Morea.

Olympia: The Temple of Hera

OLYMPIA

Olympia, in the western Peloponnese, lies in the peaceful pineclad valley of the River Alpheos. It gained its fame as a sanctuary of Zeus and Hera, but the site also contains a wealth of other small shrines, gymnasiums and sculptors' workshops. It was in the still extant stadium that the Olympic Games were founded, accordings to tradition, in 776 B.C., and the Greeks calculated their chronology from this date, measuring events by the Olympiad in which they occured. It is from here the sacred troch is still carried to whatever corner of the world the modern Olympiads are held in. The period of the Games was always marked by a Sacred Truce during which all the people of Greek race forgot their differences and united for a while in the spirit of Hellenism. In the Olympia Museum are exhibited unique sculptural masterpieces, such as Praxiteles' Hermes, Paeoneus' Victory, Apollo and many other art trasures.

The Olympic Flame

The Temple of Vassae, one of the best preserved temples in Greece. Its slender columns rise in solitary splendour on a plateau amid the wild mountains. Dedicated to Apollo, it was probably erected between 420-417 B.C. by Ictinos, architect of the Parthenon. It was commissioned by the people of the town of Phygalia because they believed that Apollo had delivered them from a plague during the Peloponnesian War.

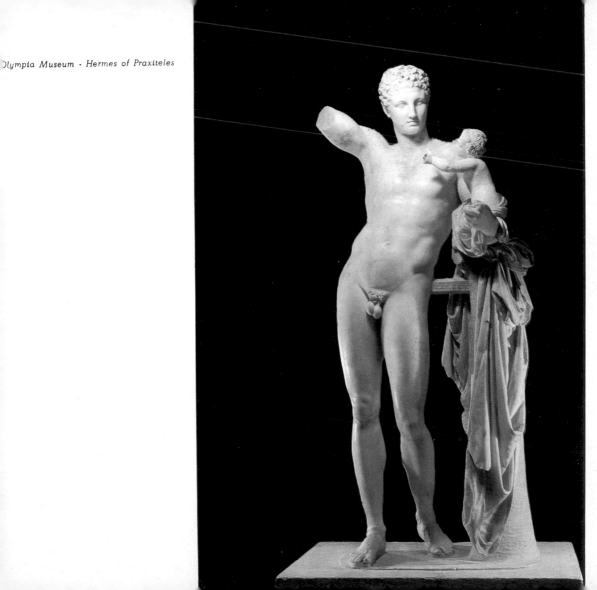

Tholos of Marmaria in Delphi

DELPHI

Delphi, was the religious centre of classical Greece. Backed by the huge crags of the Shining Rocks and looking down a wild gorge to the Gulf of Corinth, it is one of the most beautiful and awe inspiring sights in the world.

The ancient Greeks chose this unique spot for their most sacred and famed Oracle, that of Apollo, which influenced the fate of states and individuals alike for about 1000 years (7th cent. B.C. to 4th cent. A.D.), and was the greatest santcuary and spiritual centre of the world of that time. The crystalline waters of the sacred Castalia spring flow at the foot of the Phaedriades Rocks.

The sacred area also comprises an ancient theatre (3rd cent. B.C.), a Stadium and a Museum with numerous statues, among which is the masterly bronze statue of the Charioteer. It's dated c. 475 B. C.

The Temple of Apollo at Delphi.

the Charioteer

OSSIOS LOUKAS

The Monastery of Ossios Loukas (just off the Athens - Delphi road) was built by the Emperor Romanos in the 11th century A.D. in honour of a local saintly hermit who had prophesied his capture of Crete. The most interesting of its buildings is the main church, with its mosaics, rich furnishings and variegate marble floors. The mosaics are considered equal to those of Daphni and Constantinople.

Osios Loukas.

DODONI

Dodoni (Epirus). Here stood great shrine of Zeus «who gove Dodoni of the two winters» a whose oracle second only to Del in importance, was probably the m ancient in Greece.

The voice of the god was said to heard in the leaves of the sac oak. The great theatre attached the shrine is slightly larger, ev than that of Epidavros.

The theatre of Dionysus

Yannina: the mosque of Aslan Pasha

YANNINA

Yannina, capital of the Epirus and fourth city of modern Greece, stands on a legendary lake in whose waters are mirrored the imposing Castro (Citadel) on its rock and the Aslan Aga mosque beneath which, following a barbarous custom, seventeen women were put to death in 1801. It was a cultural and commercial centre even under the Turks, especially renowned for its gold and silver smiths. At the turn of the eighteenth century the notorious Ali Pasha made so powerful that the Sultan was obliged to move against him to reestablish central authority in 1822. It was Ali's mistress, the Lady Phrosyne who met her death in the waters of the lake. Close to Yannina is the Perama cave, famous, for its beautiful stalactites.

Ioannina: Perama Cave

METEORA

The dramatic rock outcrops of the Meteora (the name means' suspended between sky and earth) tower over the plain of Thessaly close to the little town of Kalambaka. Dizzily perched on these fingers of stone are 24 monasteries and convents, of which only four are inhabited today. They contain many artistic treasures and rare old manuscripts. The 16thc. convent of Roussanou (below) is noted for its fine murals. Until the end of the last century the asscent to it was made by rope ladder.

Meteora

MOUNT ATHOS

Located on a headland on the easternmost of the Chalkidiki peninsula in Macedonia, Mount Athos (Holy Mounain) constitutes the only entirely monastic state in Europe. Its 20 fortress-like monasteries and countless hermitages scattered overrugged and dramatic countryside contain many tare objects of Byzantine art and priceless manuscripts. No women or youths under 21 (except theological students) are allowed to go there.

A monk at the Mount Athos

Orestias Lake

EDESSA

Edessa (Macedonia) perched over 1000 ft. above sea level commands an exquisite view of the northern plains. Criss-crossing it are the streams the unite to form the famous falls. The water tumples 82 ft., between cliffs covered with a riot of rich vegetation, vines, figs, pome- granate and walnut trees.

CASTORIA

Castoria stands on a promontory that juts out into the beautiful Lake Orestias. Built on the ruins of the city founded by Justinian in the 6th c. A.D., it is a colourful town containing many old aristocratic mansions, richly painted and ornamented with fine carved woodwork. There are also 72 very old churches, of which the Panayia Kouveliotissa is one a charming little church, of triconic plan, decorated in squares around the dome.
The inhabitants of the town, where a fur industry flourishes, are noted for their hospitality

Edessa: falls

Thessaloniki: The White Tower

THESSALONIKI

Thessaloniki, the lively modern city overlooking the lovely Gulf of Thermai is the capital of Macedonia and second city of Greece today. St. Paul preached here, and the wealth of 14th c. Byzantine churches testifies to the heights to which Cristianity then attained in the city. Along the sea promenade the White Tower, last remainder of the 15th c. fortifications has become Thessalonikis unofficial emblem. Close to it, an International Trade Fair is held every September which is one of the most important industrial events in the Eastern Mediterranean.

THE GREEK ISLANDS

Whatever direction you take across the Aegean, there is always some island rising across the horizon. Whether wild and green, like the northern islands (Thasos and the N. Sporades), stark and sheer like the southern islands (the Cyclades), or cultivatedly luxuriant like the eastern group (Mytilene, Chios, Samos), they all have the same air of suspended time, the same little whitewashed clurches, the same pack-donkeys pacing the cobbled streets, the same fishing boats placidly riding in the harbour with great eyes painted on their prows just as they were thousands of years ago. Apart from the groups already mentioned, to the south-east is the Dodecanese, a rope of twelve islands strung against the Turkish coast, with Rhodes, the largest and most lustrous, for its clasp. Farther south still is the greatest and most complex of all the islands, Grete, a microcosm of the whole range of Greek scenery, inhabited by a fiercely independent people, almost a race apart. Everywhere one is reminded of the richness of the past by ancient cities and temples, mediaeval castles, Byzantine monasteries. For those who want a gay social life, there are bright, busy islands like Mykonos (Cyclades) and Hydra (Saronic Gulf), for those who want to withdraw into nature and forget the existence of the rest of the world, there are isolated, peaceful islands like Ios (Cyclades). Nor must we forget the western islands, the Ionian group headed by Corfu, with their more Adriatic beauty, and that strange legacy of English rule, the only regular cricket team in the whole Mediterranean. Whichever island you choose, one thing is certain. You will everywhere be dazzled by the same penetrating light and turquoise sea which have made their beauty legendary.

Hydra with its small harbour

Hydra, the long stark rocky island in the Saronic gulf, has many stately partician houses built during a period of maritime wealth in the mid-19th c. A considerable colony of foreign artists has settled there bringing an admixture of cosmopolitanism to the islands natural simplicity.
In high summer it is one of the social centres of the Aegean.

MYCONOS

Myconos, one of the mo[st]
popular tourist resorts, is [a]
small bare island from wh[e-]
re caiques cross to Del[os]
(1/2 hr. trip.) It is famo[us]
for its many windmills a[nd]
its 365 churches and ch[a-]
pels, many of which we[re]
dedicated by shipwreck[ed]
sailors. There are seve[ral]
good beaches, and in t[he]
summer nightlife is ve[ry]
lively.

PAROS

Paros, the gentlest of
the Cyclades' famous
since classical times
for its marble quar-
ries. It has fine bea-
ches, and the little
harbours hum with
the activity of the
fisherfolk.

the island of Paros

Lions of the Naxians in Delos

DELOS

Delos, the hub of the circle from which the Cyclades take their name. This tiny island, now deserted, was the most sacred in ancient Greece and honoured as the birthplace of Apollo and his sister Artemis. The ruins of the shrines and the great commercial centre that grew up around them cover the island. The famous marble lions an offering by the island of Naxos, line the Sacred Way leading to the main temples.

Mykonos : Paraportiani

SANTORINI

Santorini (or Thira) is one of the most interesting islands of the Cyclades. It is visited by numberless foreigners and Greeks every summer, who flock there to admire the extraordinary landscapes that have been created by its volcano and by earthquakes.

On the island there flourished a local civilization dating back to prehistoric times. The ruins of that civilization are buried under thick blankets of lava.

The large island of Thasos.

THE N. SPORADES

Skiros, Skopelos, Skiathos and Alonissos form a little archipelago to the north of Euboea. Both Skopelos and Skiathos are very verdant, and the latter is essentially a fisherman's island, with a charming sheltered port and a tradition of boat-building. The bay at Koukounaries (right), which takes its name from the sweet-scented pines that fringe its sweeping golden sands, is one of the most beautiful natural beaches in the whole Mediterranean.

Koukounaries at Skiathos.

Parga, a very pleasant little town on the coast of Epirus. It is built next to a picturesque bay with a magnificent sandy beach.

Corfu island

Rhodes : the port entrance

DODECANESE

The name «Dodecanese'» means «Twelve islands», (there are actualy thirteen). The best-known of these are Rhodes, Kos, and Patmos, famous both for their natural beauty and for their classical mediaeval monuments. Kos was the home of Hippocrates father of European medicine, and legend has it that the great plane tree stil growing near the mosque is the very one under which he sat to dispense his medical advice. Patmos is renowned as the place to which in 95 A.D. St. John the Divine was banished, and where he wrote the Book of Revelations. The monastery there contains many valuable possessions. Attractive among the smaller islands is Symi, lying in a bay of the Turkish coast. In its port there is a Byzantine castle and a church with frescoes. But the main island of the group is, of course Rhodes, famous in classical times for the Colossus, one of the seven wonder of the ancient world, which bestrode the entrance to its harbour. The deer, poised on their narrow columns, have become the emblems of the island since mediaeval times. Aside from the town of Rhodes itself with its turkish and mediaeval flavour, there are exquiste classical ruins at Kamiros and Lindos.

Rhodes the Palace of the Grand Masters.

Rhodes: The sanctuary of Athena on the acropolis at Lindos,

Lindos, on the south-east coast of Rhodes, was the ancient capital of the island before the town of Rhodes itself was founded. The temple of Athena on the promontory above the town stands within the walls of a Frankish castle, and looks down on one side to a pretty bay, on the other to a lagoon.

Kos, sanctuary of Asklepios, god of Medicine.

KNOSSOS

Knossos is a picturesque spot near Heraklion, Crete. A town flourished there in very ancient times (3rd-1st millenium B.C.) and it was the kingdom of Minos, the prehistoric ruler of the seas. It was the first spark of European civilization, the Minoan.

Today the visitor will see the restored ruins of Minos' palace, unearthed in 1900 by the British archaeologist Evans.

The many - storeyed palace was the centre of a big tree-surrounded town without protective walls.

Built in the 19th Century B.C. it was destroyed by earthquake and rebuilt in the 17th Century B.C.

Its complex architecture, its lordly chambers and staircases, its perfect baths with their drainage system, its masterly wall paintings, statuettes, precious jewels and carved vases, all compel the visitor's admiration.

The royal thron-room, in the N.W. corner of the main courtyard. The frescoes show mythological birds symbolising the royal power. The throne of Minos itself again bears the bull motif. Around the walls runs a stone bench where the elders sat.

◄ The Prince with the lilies, also known as the Priest — king, is one of the bas-relief frescoes in the palace of Minos at Knossos. It shows the typical portrait of a Cretan noble, bare-chested and muscular, but wasp - waisted and with long black curled hair.

Knossos: the Chamber of the Throne.

Knossos: King Minos' palace

Minoan Palace of Knossos.

Heraklion.

Aghios Nicolaos.